ENDURING VISIONS
1000 Years of Southwestern Indian Art

An Exhibition Produced
for
The Aspen Center for the Visual Arts
by
Philip M. Holstein and Donnelley Erdman

This publication has been prepared under a grant from
The Graham Foundation for Advanced Studies in the Fine Arts

Inquiries should be addressed to
The Aspen Center for the Visual Arts
Box 4449, Aspen, Colorado 81611

First Printing 1979

Distributed by
The Publishing Center for Cultural Resources,
152 West 42nd Street,
New York, N.Y. 10036

Selection of items by Philip M. Holstein

Photography by Gail Wanman Holstein,
with the exception of plates 1, 7, 9, 14,
71, 72, 74, 79, 94 and 104.

Designed by Donnelley Erdman

Type set in Chelmsford and Chelmsford Demi-Bold by
Aspen Typesetting, Aspen, Colorado

Color Separations by Gazlay Graphics, Inc., Kansas City, Mo.

Printed in the United States of America by
The Jarvis Press, Denver ● Dallas

Library of Congress Catalog Number: 79-52784

International Standard Book Number: 0-934324-00-X

Cover illustration
Hopi "Wolf" Kachina
Pueblo, ca. 1880-1900
Painted wood
40 cm
Millicent Rogers Museum

Contents

Acknowledgments

Some time ago, while discussing the possibility of organizing an exhibition of Southwestern American Indian art, it became clear that there were too few printed references on the subject. It was therefore decided that while assembling objects for the show, a catalogue might be prepared which would also serve as a beautifully illustrated "primer."

The texts which accompany each section try to give a sense of how art was interwoven with community and individual life. They also deal with aesthetic and symbolic design elements. Tony Berlant, Larry Frank and Jonathan Holstein, each known for his thorough connoisseurship, have previously written articles and books on Indian art. Jerold Collings and Joe Ben Wheat are recognized as being the most knowledgeable people in their respective fields of basketry and textiles. William Wroth, who oversees the collections at the Taylor Museum, has recently published a scholarly work on New Mexican jewelry.

Both this publication and an exhibition which opened in Aspen and travelled to the University of Colorado Museum at Boulder and the Taylor Museum at the Colorado Springs Fine Arts Center were organized by Philip and Gail Holstein and Donnelley and Cinda Erdman, who together possessed the desire and expertise to select and photograph the material as well as to design, edit, and prepare all elements of the publication. Their contribution to the Center and this project is immeasurable. Special acknowledgement for support in all phases of executing the exhibit must be given to the Board, staff and volunteers of the Aspen Center for the Visual Arts. Jill Richards has been especially helpful.

Without the financial assistance of the Graham Foundation for Advanced Studies in the Fine Arts, this idea would never have been realized. Similarly, the advice and assistance of Lorenzo Semple, Jr., and the Colorado Council on the Arts and Humanities have been essential.

The following individuals and institutions have generously allowed material from their collections to be photographed for this publication and lent to the exhibition:
Anthony Berlant
Mr. and Mrs. Lee Cohen
The Collings Collection
Cinda and Donnelley Erdman
Mr. and Mrs. Forrest Fenn
Mr. and Mrs. Larry Frank
Jonathan and Philip Holstein
Mr. and Mrs. Dennis Lyon
Joanne and Lee Lyon
Mr. and Mrs. Charles F. Murphy, Jr.
Mr. and Mrs. Robert Musser
Mr. and Mrs. Gerald P. Peters
Christopher Selser Collection
Leslie and Gary Troyer
Joe Ben Wheat Collection
The Denver Art Museum, Denver, Colorado
Denver Museum of Natural History, Denver, Colorado
The Heard Museum, Phoenix, Arizona
Millicent Rogers Museum, Taos, New Mexico
School of American Research, Santa Fe, New Mexico
The Taylor Museum at the Colorado Springs Fine Arts Center, Colorado Springs, Colorado
Museum of New Mexico, Laboratory of Anthropology, Santa Fe, New Mexico
University of Colorado Museum, Boulder, Colorado

Philip Yenawine
Director
Aspen Center for the Visual Arts

Introduction

Enduring Visions has two meanings: one for the Southwestern Indian who created this extraordinary artistic tradition; and another, quite different but no less interesting, for other peoples who have been influenced by it. Said Jackson Pollock in the 1950's: "The Indians have a true painter's approach in their capacity to get hold of appropriate images...their vision has the basic universality of all real art."[1]

While Pollock's insight is admirable, it holds a certain irony in that no Indian would have perceived his approach as painterly. Art for the Indian was simply a reflection of life; there was no distinction between the utilitarian and spiritual aspect of the blanket, the basket, the ritual figure. The Indian believed he literally sprang from the Earth; she was the great mother he both loved and feared. His materials were equally part of the Earth, and thus artifacts were physical manifestations of cosmology, a method of perpetuating mystical visions over generations. These visions symbolized things about to happen, or things which had happened and put life into perspective. The Indian artist translated his visions into motifs which celebrated the central themes of his belief: oneness and peace, the all-embracing harmony of man and his environment.

Europeans and non-Indian Americans were essentially unaware of this background when they discovered "primitive" art late in the 19th century. The vast collections assembled by European museums evoked responses not unlike Pollock's: that is to say, viewers reacted to compelling aesthetic qualities of seemingly unsophisticated artifacts.

During the 1920's and 30's, the influence spread in curiously diverse ways. Southwestern and other non-European indigenous motifs were soon adopted into the "Art Deco" style, originally an attempt to produce a streamlined, machine-like art using primitive sources. The zigzag terraced figure common to many early cultures found itself wed in the Radio City Music Hall to the segmented circles of the Hopi cloud symbol. High art becomes commerce.

Frank Lloyd Wright also partook of the vision. Wintering at Taliesin West, his atelier near Phoenix, he lived and worked in a desert environment much akin to that of the Indian. Though Mayan architecture is recognized as a major influence on his work of the 20's, Wright's personal interests in Southwestern Indian art were reflected in the classic Navajo blankets he collected and recommended to clients as wall hangings.

Many other instances of the vision's influence could be cited, but all have one thing in common: what we have taken from Indian art has always been the form, without any necessary comprehension of the content. There have been signs, recently, that this may be changing.

Ceremonial dance rituals of the Pueblo and Hopi were characterized in 1975 by Vincent Scully, the noted art and architectural critic, as "the most profound works of art yet produced on the American continent."[2] Is it possible that such an evaluation has led to a new area of creative exploration by conceptual artists?

Much of the work by the so-called "earth artists" seems to reflect a certain knowledge or respect of Indian ritual. It is not by accident that this activity is focused on the Southwest.

Perhaps the wheel turns full circle at last. As we have already observed, there was never an art which celebrated the harmony of Man and Earth, the conjunction of form and content, more resonantly than that of the Southwestern Indian. The application of this theme to the necessities of the 1980's scarcely requires comment. The vision endures...

1. Francis V. O'Connor, *Jackson Pollack*, Museum of Modern Art, N.Y., 1967, page 32.

2. Vincent Scully, *Pueblo—Mountain, Village, Dance*, Viking Press, N.Y. 1975, page xi

Gail Wanman Holstein
Philip M. Holstein

Cinda Wheeler Erdman
Donnelley Erdman

Maps

Plan locations for **Prehistoric Cultures** indicate the first or primary excavation site for a pottery type, and not necessarily the only site where it is to be found. There are few, if any *pure* prehistoric sites, as the tribes seem to have traded freely among themselves, finding pleasure and value in artifacts produced by groups whose ceramic traditions were quite different from their own. As a result, ceramics are often discovered several hundred miles from their *name site*, and it is not unusual for examples from many cultures to be found at any given archaeological site. It is for this reason that Casas Grandes pottery, not included because of its northern Mexican origin, has been found in both Arizona and New Mexico. Dates indicate the time period during which the particular tribes or cultures flourished and significant design traditions in ceramics were developed. Culture groups are shown in larger type, however all tribes in the general area defined need not belong to that group.

• MESA VERDE
1100-1300

• SIKYATKI
1400-1625

• KAYENTA
1100-1300

ANASAZI

• CHACO
950-1150

JEDDITOH •
1100-1300

FOURMILE •
1350-1400

• BIDAHOCHI
1300-1400

MOGOLLON

SNOWFLAKE •
975-1100

• ST. JOHNS
1100-1200

SINAGUA

• KINISHBA
1050-1350

TONTO •
1250-1400

SALADO

• TULAROSA
1100-1250

• RESERVE
950-1150

HOHOKAM

GILA •
1250-1400

MIMBRES

• MESA VERDE
1100-1300

• SIKYATKI
1400-1625

• KAYENTA
1100-1300

CHACO •
950-1150

ANASAZI

• JEDDITOH
1100-1300

FOURMILE •
1350-1400

• BIDAHOCHI
1300-1400

1100-1200

1250-1400

TULAROSA •
1100-1250

SALADO

• RESERVE
950-1150

HOHOKAM

GILA •
1250-1400

MIMBRES

Historic Cultures

UTAH

COLORADO

•Salt Lake City

•Denver

UTE

•Colorado Springs

San Juan River

NAVAJO

•TAOS
•SANTA CLARA
•SAN ILDEFONSO
COCHITI• •TESUQUE
Santa Fe
ZIA•
SANTA ANA• •SANTO DOMINGO

•Albuquerque

CHEMEHUEVI

HAVASUPAI

HOPI

Colorado River

Little Colorado River

Flagstaff•

ZUNI•

LAGUNA•
ACOMA•

MOHAVE

ARIZONA

NEW MEXICO

YAVAPAI

Salt River

Rio Grande River

Phoenix•

Gila River

Gila River

EASTERN
APACHE

YUMA

MARICOPA

PAPAGO

•Tucson

PIMA

WESTERN
APACHE

Painted and Sculptural Objects

Traditional native arts flourish in but a few areas of North America. Of these, the Southwest is certainly the most prolific. There, Indian craftsmen, many of whom still inhabit their ancient homelands, produce pottery, weaving, jewelry, baskets and sculpture, practicing all the crafts developed by their ancestors. In this vast area there evolved several distinct painting and sculptural traditions. Most important is that of the Puebloans, whose ancestors were the Mogollon and Anasazi. There is also that of the Yumans, derived from the Patayans, and the Pima and Papago, descendants of the Hohokam. The later-arriving Navajo and Apache, related to each other by language and their previous less settled way of life, each added a distinct sensibility to the native art of the Southwest.

While contact between the newcomers and the Pueblo peoples was often abrasive, there was also peaceful interaction; in either case important cultural exchange took place. This exchange was, in terms of development of the arts, somewhat one-sided—the foragers learning from the settled peoples the techniques of weaving, pottery, and basket making. The Navajo assimilated all these skills, though it was in weaving textiles that they eventually excelled, while the Apache became masterful only in basketmaking, another weaving art. Although techniques and some styles were adopted, both the Navajo and Apache worked them to create forms distinctly their own. In general, Pueblo styles influenced the Navajo more than the Apache.

The following is an outline of native Southwestern sculpture and painting of the later historic period. While not in any sense complete, it gives a general view of these two creative activities during the later nineteenth and twentieth centuries.

SHRINE FIGURES Pueblo shrine figures of stone and wood are used in kivas, caves, the open air—anywhere a shrine is established. They are permanent or semi-permanent fixtures at these shrines, and show a considerable variety and a remarkable continuity in form and embellishment with Anasazi and Mogollon figures. They are monumentally conceived, as is most Pueblo sculpture. Identifying features are struck from large masses with a minimum of manipulation or embellishment: scant modelling of limbs, restrained carving, painting or inlaying of abstracted characteristics (a mountain lion's tail lies along its back, a wildcat's tail is short and stubby, a girl ready for marriage wears a particular hairdo, etc.). At Santo Domingo, Cochiti and other Rio Grande Pueblos, shrine figures are made of wood and both hard and soft stones. Some figures are conical, with eyes and mouth in turquoise inlay or incising. Others are more elaborate, with a head, and perhaps limbs, carved from the shaft. Shrine figures from any pueblo may have embellishments of cloth, feathers, turquoise, shell necklaces, or other materials.

FETISHES "Fetishes" is used here in the sense of magical objects of small scale, usually made for personal, rather than clan or tribal use. They bring luck in the hunt or war, help cure, diagnose or ward off illness, protect livestock, insure fertility, or perform other functions. Fetishes may be of almost any material or construction, though carved stones predominate. Many Pueblo stone fetishes are exactly like shrine figures in form. The most famous have been made by the Zuni, who carved for themselves and other Indians such as the Navajo, and, in recent times, for tourist sale. These small stone carvings often have turquoise, feathers, arrowheads or other material attached with sinew or leather. The Zunis have also made carved antler fetishes in the form of the *Avanyu*, the great serpent deity of the Southwest, for ritual use and sale. At Taos, fetishes are made of clay and adobe in the form of "mother corn," buffalo, elk and other creatures. An occasional animal fetish shows extraordinary grace and that precise feeling for natural postures of animals which appears in much American Indian art (Plate 27).

Other Pueblos have made stone fetishes in conical or more complicated forms. These are, like those of the Hopi and Zuni, often miniatures of larger shrine figures. The Navajo make small figures of wood which are used in curing rituals. One type is humanoid, sometimes inlaid with shell or stone or having other attachments. The Apache fashioned fetishes of leather embellished with painting or beadwork, more similar to Plains than Pueblo styles.

KACHINAS   The Kachina cult was predominant in the ritual life of many Pueblo groups, but the Hopi most elaborated it; their cyclical Kachina ceremonies are justly famous. The dancers in these rituals personify individual Kachinas or deities in the large Southwestern pantheon of spirit beings. Proper attention to them is necessary to maintain the harmony of the universe. Carved wooden Kachina figures, painted with specific identifying features, have been made for a long period, perhaps since prehistoric times. They seem now to have no specific ritual function, but instead are kept in the home to remind family members of the attributes of different Kachinas.

Among the Hopi, the earliest figures were of a flat type—the head differentiated from the body by side notches, with eyes and mouths painted on in triangles and rectangles, and arms crossing the body at the abdomen. In many features they are similar to prehistorc ritual figures, from which they may have derived. The form survives in those flat Kachinas made for young children. Hopi Kachinas evolved stylistically during the later nineteenth and twentieth centuries from those simple, abstracted forms, to the beginnings of modelling, and finally to today's highly realistic and meticulously-painted figures, many of which are made for sale to non-Indians.

Zuni Kachinas of the later nineteenth and early twentieth centuries differ from those of the Hopi in the following ways: They are more realistically conceived, elongated,

rather than blocky. Clothing is usually real rather than painted, and arms are often articulated. The last two features are the rule for Zuni Kachinas (Plates 6-10) and more the exception for Hopi. The Zuni have been much less involved in making Kachinas for sale.

The rarer Kachinas of some of the Rio Grande Pueblos are stylistically similar to Hopi figures, though often made of a harder wood (Hopi Kachinas are normally cottonwood), and more simply painted. The neighboring Pueblos of Acoma and Laguna make simple columnar figures, very similar in general form to the earliest Hopi Kachinas (Plate 16). They can be flat, oval or round in cross-section, the heads divided from the bodies by incised lines, the faces painted in single colors, the eyes and mouths shown as black triangles and rectangles. Some are more elaborately decorated.

RITUAL EQUIPMENT   Many Pueblo tribes have made sculptural ceremonial equipment—Kachina dance masks with leather or wooden crests, hand-held objects for dance rituals, such as painted wands (Plate 25), screens and altars for kivas, many of which have associated carvings (snakes, flowers, birds, etc.). The Navajo also make altars with carved accessories.

SCULPTURE IN CLAY   For all the intense Pueblo interest in fired clay, which included specially shaped and decorated ceremonial vessels, there were proportionately few figurative ceremonial objects made in this medium. Zuni, Acoma, Laguna, Cochiti, Tesuque, Taos, and other Pueblos made figures or vessels in animal form. The Cochiti made large and small standing human figures, often called ''singers'' because of their stance (Plate 26); and human figures were made at other Pueblos, including Hopi. While such figures may originally have served some ceremonial function, they have, in modern times, been made for sale. The familiar Zuni owls and Acoma figures are typical examples. The figures generally emphasize body mass, have relatively small heads, and are often vigorously and charmingly painted.

The Mohave, Yuma, and Maricopa made solid clay figures—men, women, children, and often adults in cradles—the last perhaps originally of some ritual purpose similar to that served by the Kachina-cradle figures of the Puebloans (Plate 15). The figures are often very expressive, boldly painted and clothed in Yuman-style garments (Plate 30). These tribes also made pottery vessels which incorporated human features.

PAINTED HIDES AND SHIELDS Painted hides apparently were not a strong Southwestern tradition. Perhaps woven blankets of various materials fulfilled the practical function of hide robes. Some hides from Taos and other Pueblos show a decided Plains influence attributable to the Southern Plains Indians who came there for trade fairs. The Apaches, however, painted hides in their distinctive style for magical use. In recent times the Hopi have made, for sale, painted hides with Kachina motifs.

The painted shield, on the other hand, is an ancient Southwestern tradition. Depictions appear on early rock engravings and paintings, and in early murals. The basic native type is round, painted with both geometric and representational devices. While Plains-type shields have been found at some Pueblos, a result of early contact with Southern Plains Indians, the Pueblo type differs in several ways: It is generally larger, rarely has an accompanying cover, is sometimes made of two layers stitched together (perhaps an adoption from Spanish shields), and the drawings are more generally symbolic. Many shields from a given pueblo will be similarly painted, whereas Plains shield designs are highly individualistic—dream-derived by the owner or created for him by a shaman. A common pueblo decorative scheme was a thick horizontal bar with circular or rectangular motifs dividing the shield, with horns above the bar and lines projecting obliquely below (Plate 22). Depictions of *Avanyus*, bears, and other figures are also common (Plate 17). Navajo shields relate more to Plains than to Pueblo types, favoring celestial features, often on a black background, and traditional representations of animals. Apache shield covers sometimes employ realistic images, but more often feature their unique other-worldly geometric designs (Plate 21).

PAINTED MASKS The painting on Pueblo masks is often very elaborate and colorful, employing both traditional Southwestern abstractions (rain clouds, Kachina faces, etc.) and geometric figures (PLate 18). Though usually made in accordance with long-established forms, Pueblo masks gain extraordinary variety and vitality through manipulation of given structural elements and symbolic painting motifs. The Navajo make case masks in a single shape for use in their curing rituals (Plate 20). Differentiation comes largely through painting variations and the addition of simple parts. The masks are always powerful, sometimes extremely so. The Apache make case masks for their *Gan* ceremonies with elaborate crests fabricated from light, painted wooden slats, and accompanying wooden slat swords. This style is unique in North America, and points, perhaps, to a Mexican derivation.

CLOTHING AND RITUAL GARMENTS
Dance kilts of hide or cloth, with painted *Avanyu* figures and fringes of metal cones, have been made at many pueblos (Plate 23). Where Pueblo clothing was made of hide, it was often painted. The Apache developed a spare drawing style to decorate their clothing. Based in part on Southern Plains conceptions, it set restrained, thin lines of beading and painting against creamy, sometimes softly painted hides. This fine lining and coloring, in conjunction with superb cut, combine to make Apache clothing among the most elegant of American Indian garments.

Jonathan Holstein

1 Hopi Kachina
Pueblo, ca. 1880-1900
Painted wood, cotton fabric
38.6 cm
Private Collection

1

2

3

4

5

2 **Ceremonial Figure**
Pueblo, ca. 1870-1880
Painted wood, feathers
43 cm
Private Collection

3 **Hopi Shalako Kachina**
Pueblo, ca. 1900
Painted wood, feathers, cotton fabric
41 cm
Fred Harvey Fine Arts Collection,
The Heard Museum

4 **Hopi Sio Hemis Kachina**
Pueblo, ca. 1890-1900
Painted wood, cotton fabric
47 cm
Fred Harvey Fine Arts Collection,
The Heard Museum

5 **Hopi Shalako Mana Kachina**
Pueblo, First Mesa, ca. 1880
Painted wood
47 cm
Private Collection

6 **Zuni "Buffalo" Kachina**
Pueblo, ca. 1850-1875
Painted wood, feathers, buffalo hide,
tin cones
49.1 cm
Millicent Rogers Museum

6

7

8

9

10

7 Zuni Kachinas
left "Deputy" (Hututu), *right* "Longhorn"
  (Saiyataca)
Pueblo, ca. 1890-1910
Painted wood, feathers, cotton fabric,
native tanned hide
40.1 cm, 40.6 cm
Private Collection

8 Zuni "Cow" Kachina
Pueblo, ca. 1865
Painted wood, feathers, deer hide, wool
and cotton fabric, beads, metal chains,
horse hair
38.1 cm
Millicent Rogers Museum

9 Zuni Kachina (Salimopiya)
Pueblo, ca. 1890-1910
Painted wood, feathers, deer hide, cotton
fabric
40.6 cm
Private Collection

10 Zuni Kachina (Hilili Kohana)
Pueblo, ca. 1900
Painted wood, feathers, cotton fabric,
deer hide, shells
37 cm
University of Colorado Museum

11

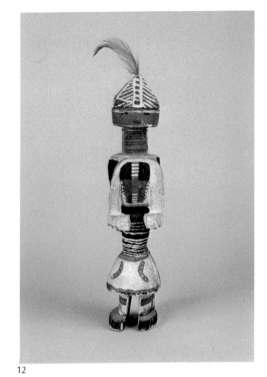
12

11 Hopi "Wolf" Kachina
Pueblo, ca. 1880-1900
Painted wood
47 cm
The Heard Museum

12 Hopi "Arrow Man" Sandpainting
  Kachina
Pueblo, ca. 1900
Painted wood, feathers
31 cm
Private Collection

13 Hopi "Snake Dancer" Figures
Pueblo, ca. 1900
Painted wood, feathers, leather
31 cm
Private collection

13

15

14

15

14 Hopi Kachina
Pueblo, ca. 1900-1920
Painted wood
35 cm
Private Collection

15 Hopi "Yellow Corn" Kachina in Cradle
Pueblo, ca. 1900-1910
Painted wood, cotton fabric, hide
31.5 cm
The Fred Harvey Fine Arts Collection,
The Heard Museum

16 Acoma Kachinas
Pueblo, ca. 1890-1900
Painted wood
25 cm
Private Collection

17 Acoma Shield
Pueblo, ca. 1820-1840
Painted buffalo leather
54 cm diameter
Private Collection

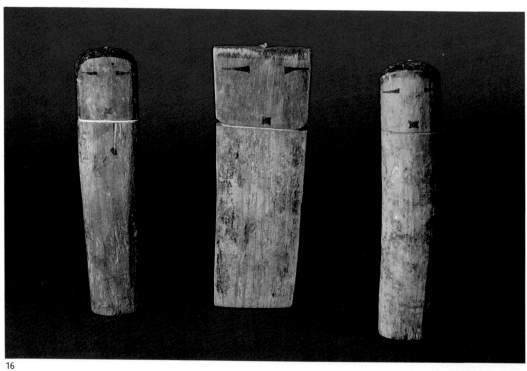

16

16

18

19

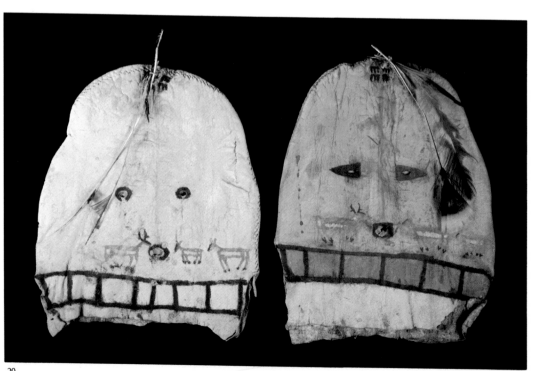

20

18 **Tableta Kachina Mask**
Pueblo, ca. 1890-1910
Painted leather and wood
50 cm high
Private Collection

19 **Kachina Mask**
Pueblo, ca. 1880-1900
Painted leather and animal skin
36.5 cm high
Private Collection

20 **Navajo Masks**
18th Century
left "Talking God", *right* "Calling God"
Painted deer hide and feathers
25.5 cm high, 29 cm high
Private Collection

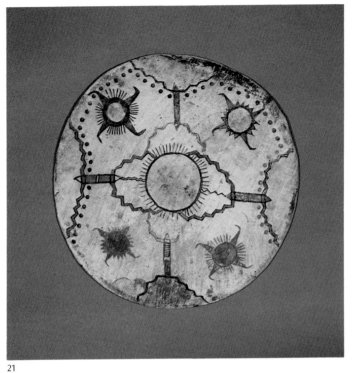

21

22

21 Apache Shield
ca. 1870-1880
Painted native tanned hide
48 cm diameter
Private Collection

22 Tesuque Shield
Pueblo, ca. 1880-1900
Painted rawhide
52 cm diameter
Private Collection

23 Teseque Dance Kilt
Pueblo, ca. 1880-1900
Native tanned leather, tin, brass cones
123 cm × 51 cm
Private Collection

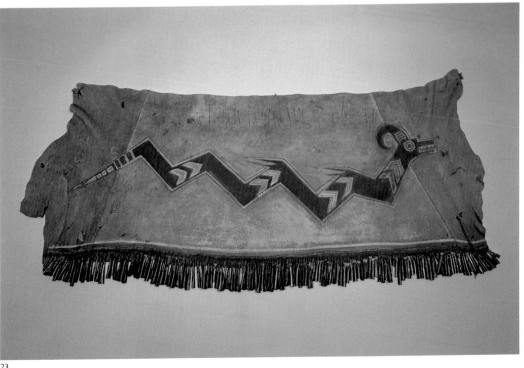

23

24

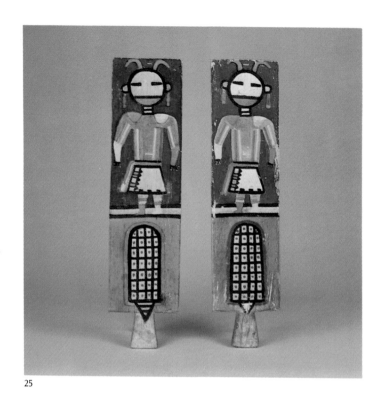

25

26

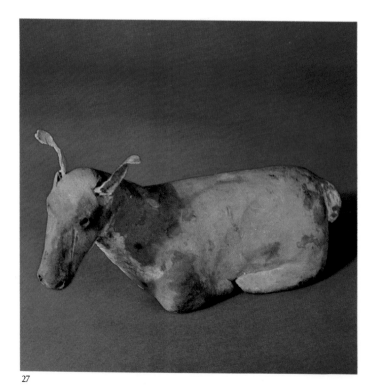

27

24 **Hopi Tableta**
Pueblo, ca. 1860-1890
Painted wood
49 cm high
Private Collection

25 **Hopi Dance Wands**
Pueblo, ca. 1900-1920
Painted wood
51 cm
The Heard Museum

26 **Cochiti Figure**
Pueblo, ca. 1890
Painted ceramic
40 cm
School of American Research,
Indian Arts Fund Collection

27 **Taos Elk Figure**
Pueblo, ca. 1880-1890
Painted adobe and leather
4.8 cm × 15.2 cm
Private Collection

28

28 **Ceremonial Figures**
Pueblo, ca. 1890-1910
Carved stone
left 15.5 cm, *right* 22 cm
Private Collection

29 **Ceremonial Figures**
Pueblo, ca. 1880-1900
Carved stone, turquoise
23 cm, 19 cm, 14 cm
Private Collection

29

30

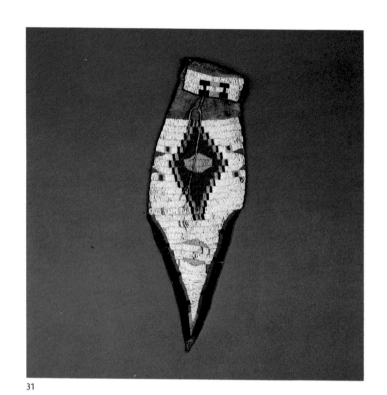

31

32

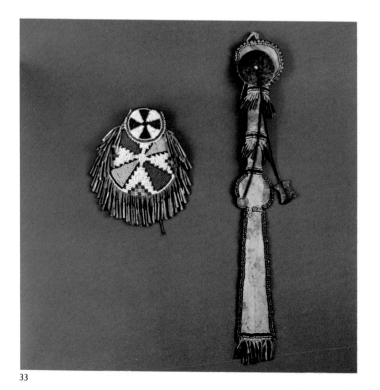

33

30 **Yuma Doll**
ca. 1880
Painted ceramic, fabric, glass beads
18 cm
Private Collection

31 **Ute Beaded Bag**
ca. 1870
Glass beads, sinew, sewn on leather
49.5 cm
University of Colorado Museum

32 **Bear Fetish with Human Face**
Pueblo, ca. 1880-1900
Carved stone
5.5 cm × 10 cm
Private Collection

33 **Apache Pouch and Awl Case**
ca. 1880
Native tanned leather, glass beads,
tin cones
16 cm, 41 cm
Private Collection

34 **Ute Cradle Board**
ca. 1880-1890
Native tanned hide, glass beads, fabric,
wood, willow reeds
104 cm
The Denver Art Museum

34

23

Weaving

By the time the Spanish Explorers discovered the American Southwest in 1540, the Pueblo Indians had been weavers of cloth for well over a thousand years. The Navajo Indians, who had arrived only a hundred years or so before the Spanish, were not yet weavers, but before the advent of the 18th century, they too were destined to become renowned for the productivity of their looms. The Spanish, who brought their own tradition of weaving to the Southwest in 1598, forever altered the course of Pueblo weaving and were instrumental in shaping the development of that of the Navajo. Through time, Pueblo, Spanish, and Navajo each influenced the other in materials and dyes, in techniques, and in design; and all achieved the summit of their art during the 19th century.

The earliest weaving of the Pueblo was done with the fingers alone, but by A.D. 800 they had developed a true loom upon which they wove a wide variety of cloths from cotton. When the Spanish settled in the Rio Grande Valley in 1598, they brought with them the long, silky-fleeced churro sheep, native to southern Spain, to provide food and wool for weaving on their own version of the European treadle loom. It was not long before yarns spun from Spanish sheep's wool were woven into Pueblo cloth on their wide, vertical loom, and dyed blue with indigo dye, which the Spanish also introduced. Pueblo weaving was forever changed. Brazilwood, logwood, and cochineal dyes came later; but threads raveled from fine English and Spanish commercial cloth provided rich, cochineal-dyed crimson yarns which the Pueblos used to decorate their cloth in weave, in embroidery, and in brocade. No more beautiful cloths have ever been cut from Southwestern looms than the Pueblo embroidered manta-dresses or shawls of the mid-19th century.

The traditional Pueblo manta, whether folded around the body to make a dress, or thrown across the shoulders as a shawl, was woven wider than long, that is, the width as measured along the weft strands was greater than the length as determined by the foundation warp yarns. In wool mantas, the center was of dark brown, undyed wool most commonly woven in plain diagonal twill, in which both warp and weft were visible. Ends were done in plain weave to facilitate application of the embroidery.

In the eastern Pueblos, the panels are usually divided into three zones—a broad-base panel, a narrower inner panel, and a row of spaced, paired figures resembling abstract blossoms without stems. In these mantas, the designs are usually developed in blocks of contrasting color, crimson and blue, or, more rarely, crimson and green or greenish-yellow. Basic elements are combinations of triangles and diamonds, joined by or flanked by more cursive geometric figures. In the base panels, these figures are usually solid embroidery in one color set against the base color of the panel, although the principal figure is frequently complemented by smaller elements done in negative outline. The narrow inner panel is normally much simpler, with a running, terraced figure in negative outline. Occasionally, a manta is found in which a monochrome panel with designs in negative outline is set above an undecorated area of plain or diamond twill. Frequently, the lateral edges of wool mantas are further embellished by a narrow line of embroidery and, very rarely, by a central, free-standing geometric motif.

Embroidered cotton mantas are usually woven entirely in plain weave, with a narrow band of decoration across the top and a much wider band across the bottom. The decorative panels are divided horizontally into three zones, and into blocks, by paired vertical stripes. Running frets in negative outline decorate the upper panel and the narrow lower zone of the bottom panel. The central, wide zone is nearly always decorated by a series of concentric diamonds in negative outline, but the center is usually left open and is embroidered with a geometric or life form, such as a butterfly or a bird. This central panel is normally surmounted by a spaced series of stacked triangles with the apex down.

The coming of the Spanish had another effect on Southwestern weaving. Many Pueblo Indians, fearful of repression by the Spaniards, fled to the Navajo homeland in the mountainous area north and west of Santa Fe. When the Navajo first appeared in history, they were hunters, farmers, and raiders, not weavers of cloth. Many Pueblo refugees were incorporated into the burgeoning Navajo tribe through the 1600s. Sometime, probably about the middle of the 17th century, the Navajos learned to weave from the Pueblos, for by the beginning of the 18th century, the Navajo had adopted the Pueblo loom and were weaving enough cloth and garments for their own use, and trading their surplus to Spanish and Pueblos alike.

Among the Pueblos, except possibly Zuni, the weavers were men; but, among the Navajo, women became the weavers. The Pueblo weaver passed the weft completely from edge to edge, leaving the cloth with an unbroken surface; but the Navajo woman knelt in front of her loom and wove her cloth in segments, leaving diagonal joints, called "lazy lines," in the web. Where the Pueblos used three cords of two-ply each for their selvages, the Navajo began to use two cords of three plies; and, where the Pueblos tended to tie off the corners loosely, if at all, the Navajo came to tie the corners tightly and to sew on an extra tassel to protect the corner. More and more, probably influenced by Spanish weaving, the Navajo wove in tapestry technique, in which the warps were hidden by the weft. It was the tapestry weave that made possible the development and efflorescence of Navajo pattern and design, for they seemingly never adopted the brocade weave or the embroidery that the Pueblo used for their most effective decoration.

Stripes were the most common form of decoration in early Southwestern weaving— Pueblo, Spanish, and Navajo alike. Stripes might be narrow or wide, simple or compound, evenly spaced over the fabric or clustered into zones, but they formed a simple and pleasing decoration. Early colors were largely confined to the natural creamy white and golden to dark brown of the churro sheep's wool, enriched by the various shades of blue derived from indigo. Later, native vegetal yellows, green, and black were added, and reds from raveled cloth or commercial yarns widened the color palate. About 1870, lavender, red, and orange aniline dyes were introduced. Complex stripes containing various figures were added to make more elaborate patterns, but stripes have never been completely replaced.

The Navajo wove many fabrics in the Pueblo wider-than-long tradition. Paramount among these were the striped shoulder blankets or "Chief's Blankets." During the 18th century, these were decorated only with alternating brown-black and white stripes of various widths. By 1800, the style known as the First Phase Chief Blanket had made its appearance. The brown end stripes had been widened and were embellished by a pair of dark blue stripes, while the black center was made much wider and had two pairs of blue stripes. In between ends and center, the man's blanket had wide alternating stripes of black and white, while the smaller, woman's blanket had narrower stripes of black and gray. Somewhat later, the blue stripes were occasionally bordered by very narrow red stripes. By mid-century, small red rectangles had been introduced into the ends and centers of each of the blue stripes, to produce the so-called Second Phase Chief Blanket. Ten years later, the Navajo began to use terraced triangles in place of the red rectangles, and by 1865 the Classic Third Phase Chief Blanket had emerged. These were marked by a central terraced diamond of red, which expanded into the field of black and white stripes, as did half diamonds in the center of each side and end, and quarter diamonds in each corner. The beauty of the Chief Blankets lies in the subtle and harmonious relation of the simple figures and the simple but dignified use of color. They were made to be worn, and the fineness of weave caused them to drape around the human form and move as the figure moved. In this they achieved their elegance.

It was on the sarape, woven in the Spanish longer-than-wide tradition, that the Navajos lavished their creative genius. Stripes were always a part of the sarape decorative scheme. One striped pattern which consists of panels of narrow, alternating, brown and blue stripes separated by wider bands of white, came to be known as the "Moki" pattern. The soft, glowing quality of the indigo blue contrasted with the silky natural brown wool to produce a fabric of subdued richness and simple beauty.

Sometime about the middle of the 18th century, the Navajo began to break away from stripes for their serapes. According to the Spanish, by 1778 they "made the best and finest sarapes that are known," and by 1880 they had fully developed the style that marked the Classic period of weaving. The terraced, or stepped-edged triangle, is the hallmark of Classic design, a style which appears to have been adapted from the designs on their basketry. Regardless of how complex a Classic blanket design may seem, it is always composed of rows or stripes of terraced triangles arranged in various ways, solid or hollow, emphasized by a rich contrast of colors. A row of triangles arranged base-to-base forms series of diamonds; arranged point-to-point, they result in rows of negative diamonds. Offset and opposed, the triangles create a negative zigzag stripe. Sometimes, hollow diamonds in white against a crimson ground are expanded into a diamond net with or without smaller diamonds inside. Occasionally, the ground consists of fine stripes instead of the solid color. Usually, the designs are arranged in a three-panel layout with large, bold figures in the center and smaller, more ordered, complex stripes across the ends. Large terraced triangles were often superimposed over the corners of the blanket, and frequently in the center of the ends, as well. Most Classic sarapes were woven in crimson from raveled cloth, indigo blue, and white with rarely a touch of black or native yellow or green. A few of these superb Classic blankets were woven as ponchos, with a slit left in the center for the head. No weaving in the Southwest has ever surpassed these fine sarapes.

The 1860s marked a turning point in Navajo weaving, when the Navajos were defeated by the American army and interned at Bosque Redondo on the Pecos River in eastern New Mexico. Here they were subjected to a variety of influences they had not experienced before. New aniline-dyed "Bayeta" was introduced, as was aniline-dyed, three-ply "Early Germantown" yarn. These new materials, combined with their handspun wool yarns, mark the blankets of the 1870s. At Bosque Redondo, the Navajo also came into contact with the serrate diamond design system that the Spanish weavers of the Rio Grande Valley had adopted from the Saltillo weavers of Mexico. These sarapes usually had a large, serrate, concentric diamond motif in the center, complex borders, and a vertically oriented layout. At first, the Navajo continued to use a side-to-side layout, but the stepped or terraced zigzags and figures gave way increasingly to serrate zigzags and figures. Borders, which had always been rare in Navajo textiles, began to enclose central dominant serrate diamond motifs. Vertical layouts increased. The new aniline-dyed commercial yarns added many previously unknown colors.

By 1875 the wedge-weave was invented, and in many ways, its large, serrate figures mark an apex of the serrate design style. Vertical zigzags, or bands of horizontal zigzags or diamonds, make it a highly distinctive textile.

From 1870 on, an increasing portion of Navajo weaving was done, not for themselves, but for others—the military, the new settlers, and finally, the tourists who began to visit the Southwest. Navajo blankets began to be used as floor covering. The transition that began about 1870, from blanket to rug, was virtually complete by 1900. The old weaving tradition ended as the new tradition of colorful Navajo rugs began.

Joe Ben Wheat
Curator of Anthropology
University of Colorado Museum

35

36 **First Phase Chief Blanket, Ute Style**
Navajo, ca. 1800-1850
Handspun native wools in natural white
and black; indigo dyed blue
142×181 cm
School of Americna Research Collections
in the Museum of New Mexico

36 **Second Phase Chief Blanket**
Navajo, ca. 1850-1865
Handspun native wools in natural brown
and white; indigo dyed blue. Red yarn
is bayeta.
134×175 cm
Fred Harvey Fine Arts Collection,
The Heard Museum

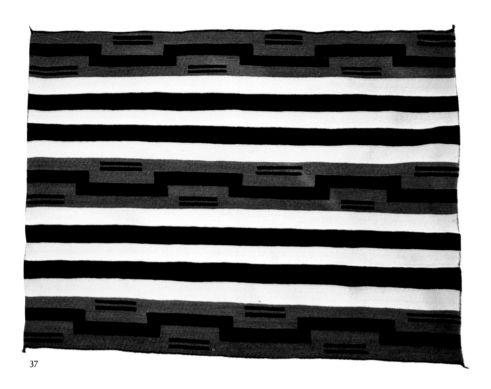

37

37 Transitional Chief Blanket, First Phase Banded Style
Navajo, ca. 1860-1870
Handspun native wools in natural white and brown; indigo dyed blue. Red yarn is bayeta.
140×178 cm
The Taylor Museum at the Colorado Springs Fine Arts Center

38 Transitional Chief Blanket, Second Phase Style
Navajo, ca. 1860-1875
Handspun native wools in natural white and brown; indigo dyed blue. Red yarn is bayeta.
134.5×178 cm
The Taylor Museum at theColorado Springs Fine Arts Center

38

39

39 Third phase Chief Blanket
Navajo, ca. 1860-1870
Handspun native wools in natural white
and brown; indigo dyed blue. Red yarn is
bayeta.
135×174 cm
University of Colorado Museum

40 Third Phase Chief Blanket
Navajo, ca. 1860-1870
Handspun native wools in natural white
and brown; indigo dyed blue. Red yarn is
bayeta, yellow is unraveled.
144× 164.5 cm
Private Collection

40

29

41

42

41 **Child's Serape**
Navajo, ca. 1840-1860
Handspun native wools in natural white
and indigo dyed blue; green is indigo with
native yellow dye. Red yarn is bayeta.
76×116 cm
Private Collection

42 **Child's Serape**
Navajo, ca. 1865-1875
Handspun native wools in natural white
and indigo dyed blue; yellow and green
are native dyes. Red yarn is bayeta, pink is
recarded.
79×119 cm
School of American Research,
Indian Arts Fund Collection

43

44

43 Child's Serape
Navajo, ca. 1840-1860
Handspun native wools in natural white
and indigo dyed blue. Red yarn is bayeta;
green is unraveled; pink is recarded.
71×130 cm
Fred Harvey Fine Arts Collection,
The Heard Museum

44 Serape
Navajo, ca. 1840-1860
Handspun native wools in natural white
and indigo dyed blue. Red yarn is Saxony.
100×166 cm
Private Collection

31

45 Serape
Navajo, ca. 1860
H.P. Mera referred to the three-ply yarns in this serape as "Zephyr." White yarn is probably three-ply silk; pink, blue, and olive green are extremely fine three-ply Saxony.
147×206 cm
School of American Research,
Indian Arts Fund Collection

45

46 Serape
Navajo, ca. 1850-1866
Handspun native wools in white and
indigo dyed blue. Red yarn is bayeta, and
olive green is unraveled yarn.
131×189 cm
School of American Research Collections
in the Museum of New Mexico

46

47 **Serape**
Navajo, ca. 1840-1860
Handspun native wools in white and
indigo dyed blue. Red yarn is bayeta.
138×193 cm
School of American Research Collections
in the Museum of New Mexico

47

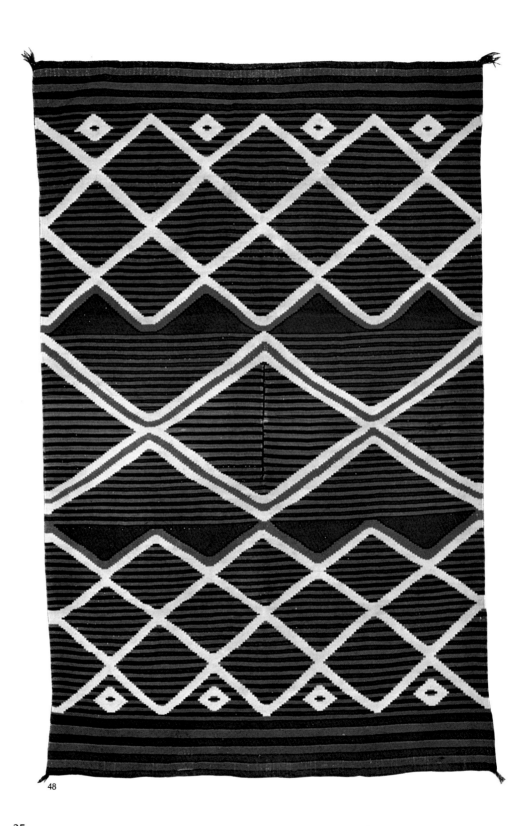

48 Poncho
Navajo, ca. 1840-1860
Handspun native wools in white and
indigo dyed blue; green is native dye. Red
yarn is bayeta.
137×190.5 cm
School of American Research Collections
in the Museum of New Mexico

48

49 Serape
Navajo, ca. 1860
Handspun native wools in white and
indigo dyed blue. The green and dark red
yarns are three-ply commercial, the
lighter red is bayeta.
113×191 cm
School of American Research Collections
in the Museum of New Mexico

49

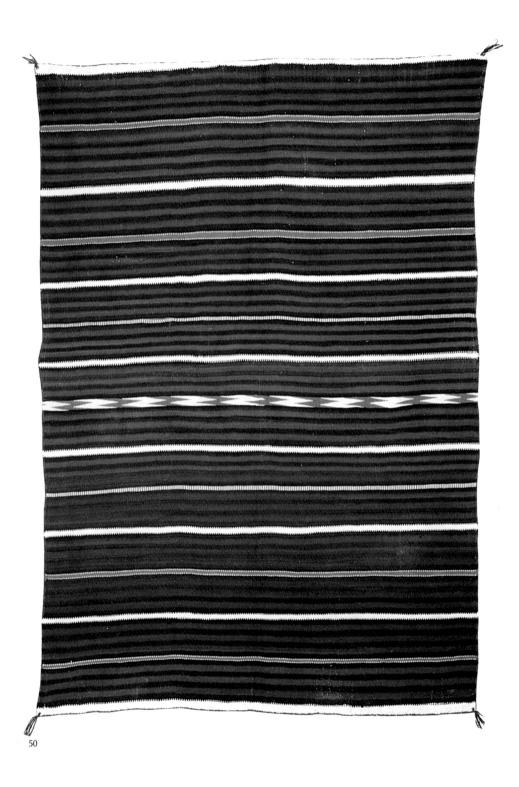

50

50 Moki Style Blanket
Navajo, ca. 1850-1870
Handspun native wools in white and brown; indigo dyed blue. Red yarn is bayeta.
119×171 cm
Collections of the Museum of New Mexico

37

51 Wedge-Weave Blanket
Navajo, ca. 1885
Handspun native wools in white and
indigo dyed blue; analine dyed red.
149×196 cm
Private Collection

51

52

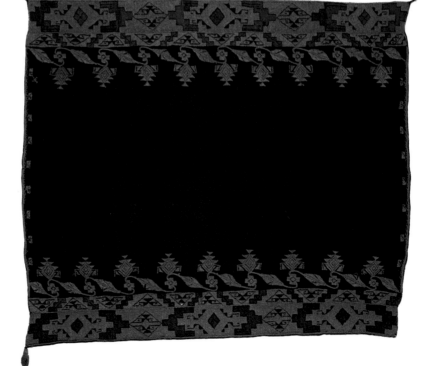

52 Hopi Ceremonial Robe
Pueblo, ca. 1890-1900
Handspun cotton yarn in white.
Commercial four-ply analine dyed yarn in
green, black, red, blue and brown.
111.5×145 cm
Private Collection

53 Acoma Shawl
Pueblo, ca. 1880-1900
Handspun native wools in natural black
and indigo dyed blue. Red yarn is bayeta.
112×145 cm
School of American Research,
Indian Arts Fund Collection

53

Baskets

The art of basket making is not new to the Southwest. For at least the past eight thousand years, Native Americans inhabiting the Southwest have been producing basketry in a variety of forms and with considerable diversification of technique. Rigid and semirigid containers, mats and bags—all played an important role in man's early attempts to cope with his strikingly beautiful but often harsh environment.

Archaeological evidence clearly establishes the prehistoric existence of all three major subclasses of basketry: twining, coiling, and plaiting. While all three of these basic techniques have been used extensively throughout the Southwest, and over long periods of time, the coiling technique has emerged as the most important tradition in Southwestern basketry. Not only does this method produce strong, durable, very closely stitched basketry, but it also offers the most potential for design development. The baskets selected for inclusion in this book will be of the coiled type.

In general, highly developed basketry is much more closely associated with the hunting and gathering cultures than with the more sedentary Pueblo groups. The principal basketry-producing tribes in the Southwest are the Western Apache and the closely associated but linguistically distinct Yavapai, the Pima and their relatives, the Papago, the Havasupai, and the Chemehuevi. One Pueblo group, the Hopi, have also made a significant basketry contribution. Of somewhat less importance, but also worthy of mention, would be the Navajo, the Ute, the Paiute, the Hualapai, the Jicarilla Apache, and the Mescalero Apache.

The traditional native basket weaver was a true folk artist. She created works that were always an inextricable part of the social, economic, and ceremonial activities of her society. She worked within a limited range of shapes and designs that had been collectively established by the society of which she was a member. Yet, even working within these imposed limitations, there was room for a high degree of individual achievement, and seemingly endless variation. It is probable that only an occasional, especially gifted individual would add her own contribution of talent or quality to the prevailing style. Thus, a new standard might be established that would become a model to be imitated by other weavers, who though perhaps less gifted, were nonetheless motivated to put forth their best effort. The effect was cumulative and resulted in the creation of basketry that both technically and aesthetically rivals the best done anywhere in the world.

One prominent early scholar, O.T. Mason, wrote, "Before the coming of the Europeans, basketry supplied nearly every necessity of the Indians, from an infant's cradle to the richly decorated funerary jars, burned with the dead. The wealth of a family was counted in the number and beauty of its baskets and the superlative virtue of woman was her ability to produce them." (Mason, 1904) A woman's ability to produce fine baskets greatly enhanced her status among her peers. Fine baskets were a form of wealth; and a woman who could produce them was highly esteemed.

Beauty of Indian basketry often goes unnoticed by observers who have grown accustomed to today's preoccupation with much slicker art. The current body of literature concerning basketry holds little in the way of discussion of the aesthetics. Such discussion as there is, is often quite casual and demonstrates a lack of depth and understanding. To put it another way, there really is no organized body of understanding that agrees on precisely how to distinguish good from bad in Southwestern basketry. There are, however, a number of points that should be considered, among which are the overall visual impact, degree of adherence to traditional form and design, the quality and preparation of the materials, the mastery of technique, and the condition.

Despite a widely held and persistent belief that cryptic meanings are associated with

Southwestern basket designs, there is little justification for this in fact. Most of the old weavers simply say the designs are to make the baskets look nice. Although they may have names for individual motifs, these names serve mainly to identify that particular design; and while it is certainly possible that some traditional design patterns may have sprung from spiritual beliefs, any such deeper meanings have been lost in time.

The designs employed by each individual tribe were sufficiently restricted so that, coupled with similar restrictions on technique and material choices, individual tribal styles can be readily recognized. Pima designs, generally, are totally integrated, forming a mosaic in which individual elements cannot be removed without destroying the design concept. Apache and Yavapai baskets tend to incorporate scattered or banded elements, while Chemehuevi designs are simple, almost spare. The use of life forms as a motif in Southwestern basketry had its origin in the prehistoric period, but it was discontinued and did not appear again until the late 19th century. Also at this time colors other than those of the traditional light and dark natural materials were introduced. This phenomenon, with few exceptions, was short lived.

The fact that native forms of basketry have survived to the present, even in severly limited quantity, is a testimonial to the tenacity with which the Southwestern Indians have clung to their native cultures. But acculturation continues to take its toll, and native customs and values continue to break down or become altered. Traditional basketry is simply no longer relevant to Indian people trying to cope with modern America. While it is probable that a few commercially adapted forms of basketry will linger on for some time, at present there seems little doubt that basketry, as a native Southwestern art form, has nearly fulfilled its destiny.

Jerold L. Collings

54 **Chemehuevi Olla**
ca. 1890
31 cm h.×38 cm diameter
Private Collection

41

55

56

57

58

42

55 **Chemehuevi Tray**
ca. 1890-1900
46 cm diameter
Private Collection

56 **Pima Tray**
ca. 1880-1900
41 cm diameter
Private Collection

57 **Pima Tray**
ca. 1850-1870
59 cm diameter
Private Collection

58 **Pima Tray**
ca. 1900-1910
42 cm diameter
School of American Research, Indian Arts
Fund Collection

59 **White Mountain Apache Olla**
ca. 1890-1910
53.3 cm h.×50.8 cm diameter
Millicent Rogers Museum

59

60

61

62

63

60 **Pima Olla**
ca. 1900-1920
44 cm h.×48 cm diameter
The Heard Museum

61. **Western Apache Olla**
ca. 1900-1920
46 cm h.×45.5 cm diameter
Private Collection

62 **Western Apache Olla**
ca. 1890-1910
44 cm h.×36 cm diameter
The Denver Art Museum

63 **Western Apache Polychrome Olla**
ca. 1900-1920
46 cm h.×34 cm diameter
The Denver Art Museum

64 **Western Apache Polychrome Olla**
ca. 1900-1920
64 cm h.×59 cm diameter
The Heard Museum

64

65

66

67

68

65 **Yavapai Tray**
ca. 1900-1920
36 cm diameter
Private Collection

66 **Yavapai Tray**
ca. 1900-1920
41 cm diameter
Private Collection

67 **Western Apache Tray**
ca. 1900-1920
44.5 cm diameter
Denver Museum of Natural History

68 **Western Apache Tray**
ca. 1890
48 cm diameter
Private Collection

69

69 **Havasupai Tray**
ca. 1920-1930
19×24.5 cm
Private Collection

70 **Navajo Bowls**
ca. 1890
29 cm diameter, 36 cm diameter,
23.5 cm diameter
The Heard Museum

70

47

Prehistoric Pottery

In the American Southwest, the Prehistoric period ends at the time of the high Renaissance in Europe, with the coming of the Spanish. For almost a thousand years before their arrival, the Pueblo Indians established an art tradition that today remains among the most profound of our national heritage.

These peaceful and industrious people were subsistence farmers and capable hunters. In many aspects they were remarkably similar in beliefs and lifestyle to their descendants who still live in the Southwest. Their pottery expresses the oneness they felt with the forces of nature. In a land of harsh living conditions, this unity was a necessity for practical as well as spiritual survival. The connection between nature and the people was strong, a bond which should be especially meaningful to us now. Their pottery grew from the earth around them, produced from their soil by their own hands. Using the simple coil technique, they built the vessels that were to become a timeless expression of their minds. The pots reveal universal truths that are seen in the pottery-making traditions of ancient peoples from many parts of the world.

The legacy of this pottery discloses a people whose art attained the highest level of abstraction, while still retaining the qualities of spontaneity and intimacy. For them, man was part of a continuum. Its perfect order and energy is nowhere better conveyed than in the mandala-like geometric images that adorned their pottery.

A great deal of technical information has been gathered by archaeologists studying these people, their dwellings, villages, economies, and migrations—but the appreciation of their pottery as art is still in its infancy. A careful study of their painting tradition will give us an understanding of their lives and mystical visions. Each vessel comes to us as a message that bridges time and vast cultural differences. The hand of the potter has revealed the ancient Pueblo world, its sense of order and organic perfection. Its art is not just about nature, but rather a manifestation of the order of nature itself. The pottery, both in its dimensional shape and its painted images, seems to have been formed by the same sense of ingrained order that directs the spider to build its crystalline web. These vessels are an expression of the Pueblo world view, while at the same time they clearly express a sense of the individual potter and her eccentricities.

The Pueblo view of life changed rapidly with the arrival of the Spanish. After the defeat of these cultures, the pottery never again carried the same absolute conviction of Pueblo cosmic identity and timelessness.

Prehistoric pots are not just archaeological data; the exact tone of voice and quality of touch of the potter, brought through time, make them illuminating works of art. In looking at these works, we come face to face with one, long-gone, but forever present. At this moment, in responding to their art, in a very real sense we assure their immortality.

These pottery images seem to span all our categories of painting, including naturalistic representation, abstraction, and non-objective imagery. Much of the painting seems to us, at least at first encounter, to be non-objective, expressing the response of the hand to the shape of the vessel, and carrying the rhythms of a life filled with energy and incredible images.

It is impossible for us to know the exact meaning that these objects had for the Pueblos. In time we come to sense that most of the designs have a symbolic as well as a purely aesthetic meaning. Most of the images fall into the area of abstraction. Every configuration seems to have had some associative value.

Often a form seems to have several simultaneous meanings. For example, one thinks of the bird tail, which is also a cloud configuration. When the bird's beak motif is presented, sometimes we see the entire animal; sometimes it is merely a spiral which represents the curving beak, which stands for the bird, which again stands for a larger concept. One jar has a painting of a human arm with a hand, which is also presented as both bear paw and rain cloud.

There seems to be a rather limited group of highly charged images, among them the bird, cloud, snake, Kachina face, and hand. These provide a format for extraordinary graphic inventions, while following established formal and symbolic canons that were to evolve over a period of hundreds of years. Within this tradition of high associative abstraction there is, above all, a sense of concentration in producing the particular objects. They never seem mechanically done; each has its own spirit and identity.

The few naturalistic images that these people produced give us very special insights about their lives. The most striking example of this information comes from the pottery of the Mimbres culture, which allows us some "realistic" glimpses of Pueblo life that would never be available in any other form.

One can see from the Mimbres bowls many of the people's activities, such as hunting and fishing practices, games, rituals and dances, and also the wide variety of wildlife that lived in the area. We also encounter, in a most spectacular manner, the supernatural creatures that dwelled only in their minds.

With few exceptions the pottery was used in what we would call a utilitarian role, although to make a distinction between the secular and spiritual is a distinctly non-Pueblo concept. These vessels were used to hold food and water, which were a gift from the spirits. An activity such as the preparation and eating of food, which we might see as prosaic, had for them great spiritual content.

They did not see these objects at a distance, propped up as embellishments to life; rather they were at hand, or in the hand. They were central and intimate containers of what was most important in their lives, both in a physical and spiritual sense.

A considerable portion of the population must have made pottery. However, it is unclear to what extent pottery making was a specialized activity. The potters were probably women, as in later historic Pueblo cultures. There was also basket- and textile-making during this time. Although few examples have survived, it is clear that the geometric tradition seen in the pottery existed in the other mediums as well. While the artisans used a limited set of geometric forms—spirals, key figures, cross-hatching, checkerboarding, stars, circles, and squares—these elements appear in endlessly varied combinations.

Central to the pottery traditions is a yin-yang sensibility. Each delineation of a form simultaneously defines the form and creates the shape of the space around it. Often the two design elements are so perfectly balanced that the separation of figures from the background seems to disappear. There are no negative spaces. So skillfully do the images fit into the concave spaces they occupy that when viewed frontally, the bowls sometimes create the illusion of being flat or convex.

The pots are immediately interesting, but their organizational complexity can be seen only after sustained contemplation. Their geometric vocabulary reflects the universal human experience.

In the Southwest, the vast desert landscape reveals the horizon in most of its 360 degrees. The world can be seen as a circle, and the sky appears to be an enormous bowl inverted over the earth, animated by clouds during the day, and by stars and the moon at night. The painted pottery is an aesthetic metaphor for the world in which it was made.

Anthony Berlant

71 **Mimbres Black on White "Story" Bowl**
Mogollon, ca. 1100-1400
23.5 cm diameter
Private Collection

72 **Mimbres Black on White Bowl**
Mogollon, ca. 1100-1400
36 cm diameter
Private Collection

73 **Mimbres Polychrome Bowl**
Mogollon, ca. 1100-1400
33.3 cm diameter
Millicent Rogers Museum

74 **Mimbres Polychrome Bowl**
Mogollon, ca. 1100-1400
30 cm diameter
Private Collection

72

73

74

75 Tonto Polychrome Olla
Salado, ca. 1250-1400
23 cm h.×39 cm diameter
University of Colorado Museum

76 Four Mile Polychrome Bowl
Salado, ca. 1350-1400
26 cm diameter
Private Collection

77 Four Mile Polychrome Bowl
Salado, ca. 1350-1400
17.5 cm diameter
Private Collection

78 Pinedale Polychrome Bowl
Salado, ca. 1250-1325
16 cm diameter
Denver Museum of Natural History

76

77

78

79

80

81

54

83 **Tularosa (or Roosevelt) Black on White Bowl**
Anasazi, ca. 1100-1350
24 cm diameter
Private Collection

84 **Mesa Verde Black on White Olla**
Anasazi, ca. 1100-1300
32.4 cm h.×32.4 cm diameter
University of Colorado Museum

85 **McElmo Black on White Canteen**
Anasazi, ca. 1100-1150
13 cm h.×26 cm diameter
Collections of the Museum of New Mexico

86 **Knishba Polychrome Bowl**
Salado, ca. 1050-1350
27 cm diameter
Denver Museum of Natural History

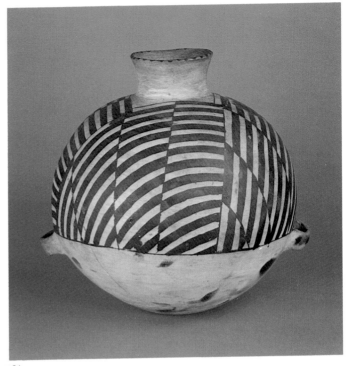
84

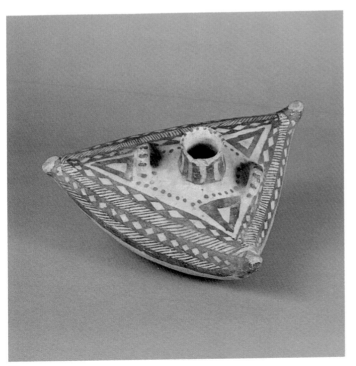
85

86

87 **Sikyatki Polychrome Olla**
Prehistoric Hopi, ca. 1400-1625
Excavated at Kawaikuh
25.5 cm h.×40.5 cm diameter
University of Colorado Museum

88 **Sikyatki Polychrome Bowl**
Prehistoric Hopi, ca. 1400-1625
Excavated at Kawaikuh
26.4 cm diameter
University of Colorado Museum

89 **Sikyatki Brown on Yellow Bowl**
Prehistoric Hopi, ca. 1400-1625
Excavated at Kawaikuh
27.2 cm diameter
University of Colorado Museum

90 **Sikyatki Polychrome Bowl**
Prehistoric Hopi, ca. 1400-1625
Excavated at Kawaikuh
29 cm diameter
University of Colorado Museum

87

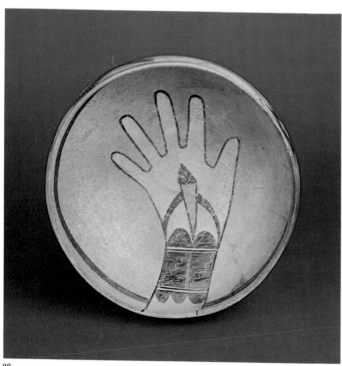

88

89

Historic Pottery

It is easy to understand why a great pottery tradition developed in the Southwest region of the United States. A sedentary, farming culture in arid lands needs pottery to store its supply of water. Pots were to hold that precious liquid and the life-sustaining grain, and their shapes and designs matched in beauty the importance of what they held.

Both Prehistoric and Historic pottery are vital expressions of the Pueblo Indians. *Prehistoric* refers to ceramics made before the arrival of Europeans in the Southwest between 1500 and 1600 A.D., and *Historic*, to that period between 1600 A.D. and the early 1920's. In the 20th century the era of contemporary pottery began, strongly influenced by the tourist trade.

When the Prehistoric Indians abandoned their sites at Chaco Canyon and Mesa Verde around 1300 A.D., they occupied the present sites of the Zuni and Hopi pueblos, from where they wandered southeast to the Rio Grande river. Here they established more villages, many of which have been continuously occupied to present times. With the arrival of the white man, Pueblo architecture, religion and ceremonies remained essentially the same, but pottery-making changed radically. Spanish priests forbade the ancient Pueblo practice of burying whole pots with the dead, and instead encouraged the Indians to use cemeteries. As a result, the Indians were forced to divert their energies primarily to the creation of utilitarian pottery for everyday domestic use. Religious pottery was made only for secret ceremonial use, to be carefully guarded in the sacred kivas.

Utilitarian pottery in particular has been passed down from family to family, and it is amazing how the older vessels have survived to our day. Historic pottery takes on a rich patina from constant handling over many generations. Sometimes the flat dough bowls, giant high-walled storage jars, smaller jars and canteens show previous repairs, but somehow have endured. Time has been kinder to Prehistoric pottery. Because it was buried in the earth, it was preserved for posterity.

It should be emphasized that all social and cultural activities of the Pueblo Indians had at least some religious significance. This certainly included pottery-making, even for utilitarian purposes. Being a deeply conservative and traditional people, the Indians employed ancient design motifs on their pottery, symbolizing rain, clouds, stars and lightning, as well as birds and animals. Here, preserved in design, was the world of nature they worshipped.

It is quite apparent that each of the nineteen pottery-producing Pueblos has a unique style. It is by design variations, and the content of the clay and slip native to each, that we can distinguish the work of one Pueblo from another. Zuni pottery is characterized by rosettes and heart-line deer, dark bases of basalt clay and a very white slip; Acoma by a profuse swirl of geometric designs and its light weight; Santo Domingo by blunt, hard-edged triangles and circles; Zia by tapestries of floral designs and the typical Zia bird ... and so it goes, each Pueblo having its own special characteristics.

Since the Pueblos traded with each other, the pottery makers often borrowed designs and incorporated them into their own traditions, creating a collective Pueblo Indian vocabulary.

The *golden age* of Historic pottery was from 1700 to 1800 A.D., when the early shapes and designs reached a zenith of expression relatively uninfluenced by European contact. A distinguishing feature of jars of this period is that they are widest in the middle, while later jars reach their maximum diameter at the shoulder. Unfortunately, few of the older pots exist today, as the first serious effort to collect Pueblo ceramics was not begun until 1880, when the Stevenson Expedition from the Smithsonian Institution visited New Mexico. Few collections were added until the 1920's, by which time the early pots were practically unobtainable. Thanks to a few far-sighted curators and collectors, we are able to appreciate Historic Pueblo Indian pottery today.

Larry Frank

91 McCartys Polychrome Jar
Acoma Pueblo, ca. 1860-1880
31 cm
Private Collection

91

92

93

94

95

92 **Ako Polychrome Jar**
Acoma Pueblo, ca. 1750
27 cm
Private Collection

93 **Acomita Polychrome Jar**
Acoma Pueblo, ca. 1820
25.5 cm
School of American Research Collections
in the Museum of New Mexico

94 **Acoma Polychrome Jar**
ca. 1900
39 cm
Private Collection

95 **Acoma Polychrome Jar**
ca. 1900-1920
31.5 cm
Collections of the Museum of New
Mexico

96

96 **Polacca (or Hano) Polychrome Jar**
Hopi, probably Nampeyo, ca. 1870-1890
18.5 cm
University of Colorado Museum

97 **Cochiti Polychrome Dough Bowl**
ca. 1900-1915
26 cm
Private Collection

97

98

99

100

101

98 **Santa Ana Polychrome Jar**
ca. 1860-1880
21 cm
Private Collection

99 **Powhoge Polychrome Storage Jar**
San Ildefonso Pueblo, ca. 1780
40 cm
Private Collection

100 **Zia Polychrome Storage Jar**
ca. 1850-1880
36.9 cm
School of American Research,
Indian Arts Fund Collection

101 **Kiua Polychrome Storage Jar**
Cochiti Pueblo, ca. 1840
50 cm
Private Collection

102 **Cochiti Polychrome Storage Jar**
ca. 1850
49 cm
Private Collection

102

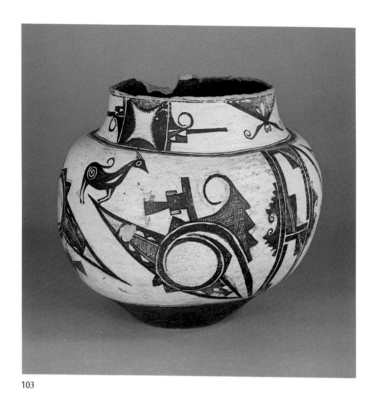

103

103 **Zuni Polychrome Jar**
ca. 1800
26 cm
Private Collection

104 **Zuni Polychrome Jar**
ca. 1870-1890
29.5 cm
Private Collection

105 **Zuni (Kiapkwa) Polychrome Jar**
ca. 1840-1870
33 cm
School of American Research,
Indian Arts Fund Collection

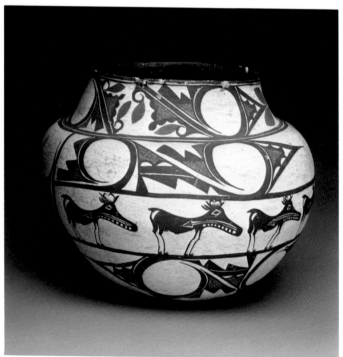

104

105

106 **Zuni (Kiapkwa) Polychrome Bowl**
ca. 1830-1850
43 cm diameter
School of American Research Collections
in the Museum of New Mexico

107 **Zuni (Kiapkwa) Polychrome Jar**
ca. 1840-1850
26 cm
Private Collection

108 **Zuni Polychrome Jar**
ca. 1900
28 cm
Collections of the Museum of New
Mexico

106

107

108

Jewelry

Love of personal adornment is an age-old phenomenon to be found in nearly every culture of the world. Among the early peoples of the Southwest and northern Mexico—the Hohokam, Mogollon, and Anasazi cultures—the making and wearing of jewelry was an important concern; beautiful objects of turquoise and other minerals, shell, bone, and vegetal substances have survived from prehistoric times, although their specific ritual uses and meanings are now lost to us.

In the historic period, the arrival of Europeans with their more technologically-complex culture signalled the possibility of major change in the art of jewelry-making in the Southwest. With the Europeans came trade items, tools, and more sophisticated methods of extracting and working minerals and metals. Iron and silver soon became more readily available, and the art of working these metals was conveyed to the native peoples. In the 1850's, it is said, the Navajo first learned the art of working iron and silver from Hispanic New Mexican smiths and soon were able to make their own bridles, bits, stirrups, and other horse equipment. Soon after this, by the early 1860's, the Navajo were also making buttons, buckles, and other simple ornaments.

In the 1870's the art of silversmithing was transmitted to the Zuni people who already, since the 1850's, had had their own blacksmiths. Independently, and again from Hispanic smiths, some of the Rio Grande Pueblos also acquired the art, making beads and cross necklaces of silver and later some silver filigree. Although the earliest documented date for eastern Pueblo silverwork is also the 1870's, it is quite possible that, due to constant interaction with the Spanish settlers since the late 16th century, they may have learned the art much earlier.

While Hispanic smiths were probably the major influence on Southwest Indian silverwork, others must also be counted. The

Plains Indians may have been working silver as early as 1800, and they traded extensively with both the Indians and Hispanos of the Southwest. Plains jewelry, itself, was in part dependent upon Hispanic Mexican prototypes, again the equestrian equipment which usually found its way to southern Plains tribes through raiding and through the work of Hispanic smiths. It was also dependent upon trade silver produced in quantity for Indian consumption by Eastern American and Canadian silversmiths. While there is at present no documentary evidence of direct Plains influence upon Southwest jewelry, it seems likely to have been a factor in the transmittal of certain popular forms such as the *concha* belt of round, and later, oval discs, and the crescent or *naja* ornament used first on horse bridles and later on necklaces. The famous Navajo *squash blossom* (Plate 112) seems to derive directly from the Hispanic pomegranate design, used as silver decorations upon the fancy trousers of the Mexican and New Mexican *caballeros* (horsemen). All of these forms have Hispanic Mexican prototypes and may have come to the Navajo both directly from the Hispanos and indirectly via the Plains Indians.

In any case it is apparent that for the Plains and the Southwest Indians the Hispanic Mexican *caballero* was both the source of many of their designs and the ideal they sought to emulate and to re-interpret in their own way. Just as the horse itself and many other cultural traits were introduced to both Plains and Southwest Indians from the Spanish pioneers, so also were items of dress and personal adornment. A description of a Pawnee chief about 1835 notes: "In his left hand he held the reins of a heavy and highly-ornamented Spanish bridle, with a curved bit, long enough to break the jaw of any horse that should venture to pull against it and which, from the gilt, stars, chains, and buckles which adorned it, seemed to have belonged to the same *caballero* of the seventeenth century as the spurs which I before mentioned."[1]

1. Feder, Norman. "Plains Indian Metalworking" (Part I), American Indian Tradition, VII, 1962, page 71

The Navajo also adapted with a passion both the horse itself and the trappings and personal adornments favored by the *caballeros*: "The Navajo ideal of splendour is the Mexican *vaquero* in gala attire, horse and rider heavily bedecked with silver."[2]

Eastern Pueblo silverwork found quite another source besides the *caballero* for its inspiration. Its most characteristic piece is the necklace of round beads interspersed with small crosses, with a pendant in the form of a large double-barrelled cross (Plate 112).

Although much has been made by many writers on the subject of the supposed resemblance of this cross to the dragonfly symbol occurring in Pueblo myths, the necklace itself is clearly based upon the Spanish Catholic rosary, and was certainly understood as such by the Pueblos who had practiced Catholicism along with their own religion since the 17th century. The rosary was introduced by the Spaniards and was a basic necessity for every New Mexican Catholic, whether Hispanic or Indian. The same style of rosary necklace is found in Mexico, particularly Oaxaca, where they are prized as heirlooms today by the Zapotec Indians; and it is likely that it was introduced from Mexico by the Franciscan friars stationed in the New Mexican Pueblos, or simply by traders. The popular double-barrelled cross pendant is a variant of the patriarchal cross with the sacred heart at its base. Similar crosses and other items were also made by Canadian and eastern American silversmiths for the Indian trade in the late 1700's and the early 1800's, and they were traded in the Great Lakes region and the Plains. They may well have found their way to the eastern Pueblos, through the Plains Indians and French Canadian trappers and fur traders, providing another possible source for this style of pendant.

In the "classic" period of Southwest Indian jewelry-making, what use and values did the jewelry have for the people themselves? For traditional peoples the desire to enhance the natural beauty of the human body ultimately finds its origin in religious concerns and practices. In fact, all material objects and natural substances have both a direct,"matter-of-fact"significance and a religious meaning: they embody cosmic and divine qualities in a material form, serving as reminders, symbols of what lies beyond the everyday world. The American Indians are particularly adept at visualizing simultaneously both the material and spiritual aspects of things.

Although silver itself was a late addition to the cultural complex of the Southwest, substances used for jewelry in pre-historic times such as turquoise, feathers, shell, bone, crystal and jet have great symbolic meaning, and they still figure prominently in Southwest cosmology and in specific ritual practices. Turquoise, later so important in Indian jewelry, is a primary symbol of the divine creative and life-giving force. Among the Navajo, turquoise is identified with the Sun—the source of life—and following from this, with the cardinal direction, south, and with the creative divinity, Changing Woman. South is the spatial direction from whence comes warmth, fertility and abundance. Changing Woman embodies and materializes the creative principle—the life-giving force of the Sun: it is the union of the Sun with Changing Woman—this personification of Mother Nature—which leads to the creation and prosperity of humankind.

In ritual life turquoise plays an important part, particularly for young women in their maiden ceremonies (*kinaalda*), to insure fertility and future prosperity. This role is pre-figured in the story of Changing Woman's own maiden ceremony in which "they dressed her in white shell shoes, fine deer-skin robes and the finest sort of shell and turquoise ornaments."[3] In their maiden ceremonies, Navajo girls symbolically re-enact the role of Changing Woman, bringing new life and fertility to their people and thereby maintaining them in the natural harmony of the cosmos. During these ceremonies they are laden with jewelry, and in the ritual

2. Woodward, Arthur. *Navajo Silver: A Brief History of Navajo Silversmithing*, Northland Press, 1971. page 85

3. Klah, Hasteen. *Navajo Creation Myth: The Story of the Emergence*. Recorded by Mary C. Wheelwright. Santa Fe: Museum of Navajo Ceremonial Art, 1942, page 76

prayers chanted at this time the connection with Changing Woman is affirmed:

Changing Woman, she moves
Her shoes of turquoise, she moves
. . .
Her belt of turquoise, she moves
Her shirt of turquoise, she moves
Her necklace of turquoise, she moves
Her earrings of turquoise, she moves
. . .
She sings: her voice is beautiful, she moves
Sahanahray Bekayhozhon, she moves
Behind her all is beautiful, she moves
Before her all is beautiful, she moves.[4]

Among the Zunis, turquoise, shell and other jewel substances play a similar important ritual role. They figure significantly in Zuni myths and are important elements in the ritual offerings to holy personages. In ceremonial dances the decorating of the body with these and other natural substances plays an essential part. Paints were prepared from sacred minerals and plants, the preparation itself an elaborate ceremony, and then were applied to the face and body in patterns having cosmic correspondences. A man whose face and body were thus painted was transformed into a sacred being with a specific ritual role to play: "Next to the mask, the face and body paint is the most sacred part of a dancer's regalia. No one must touch a man while he has on his body paint."[5] In addition to masks and paint, the dancers often wear much jewelry, strands of turquoise, shell and other substances around their necks.

Thus in the holistic perspective of the Southwest Indians, elaborate personal adornment has served since prehistoric times to fulfill ritual functions; in general it has the purpose of keeping man in harmony with the natural world and the cosmic forces around him.

In secular terms jewelry, both turquoise and silver, became for the Indians a symbol of

prosperity. It was a means, in a non-commercial society, of holding wealth, and on important occasions the wearing of much jewelry served as an indicator of one's economic position in the community. For the Navajo, like other nomadic peoples, jewelry was a particularly handy means of having easily transportable wealth.

The advent of silver, while not of great ritual significance, provided a new medium in which to create beautiful objects. Early Navajo and Zuni silver jewelry, based as it is upon male equestrian equipment, tends to be virile, massive, and heavy. The simplicity of design, the result of filing, chisel work, and minimal stamped motifs, is enhanced by the soft glowing texture of the heavy coin silver from which it was made. When turquoise was used, a few irregular, large pieces were set in deep bezels which came up level with the top of the stone. There is an unrefined quality, even crudeness, in these early pieces which actually adds to their appeal, for compared to the machine-like perfection of later jewelry they have a pleasing handmade appearance. They are simple and symmetrical, but their imperfection gives them a vitality, an organic feel that is lacking in newer, though perhaps better crafted, pieces.

These objects, although derivative from other peoples, express in their simple, harmonious forms the sense of wholeness inherent in the Navajo and Zuni cultures. They tend to be, like decorative art the world over, symmetrical and balanced, showing a fine, innate sense of proportion upon the part of the makers—the characteristic design, regardless of the form or purpose of the piece, is often concentric or bilaterally symmetrical and is focused upon a central motif. Circular and oblong forms such as buttons, *conchas*, and *ketohs* are especially centralized, with all elements leading to or otherwise in harmony with the center. Such pieces reflect quite naturally the Indian sense of spatial organization, in which everything proceeds in an ordered fashion from and

4. Klah, op. cit., page 153

5. Bunzel, Ruth L. "Zuni Katchinas: An Analytical Study," in 47th Annual Report of the Bureau of American Ethnology, Washington: United States Government Printing Office, 1932, page 868

returns to the central originating point.

A different design style, not quite so common, is the overall geometric pattern, or its variant the repeated motif, both of which lack a central focus. These patterns are most usually found on the earliest silver pieces before the setting of turquoise came into practice after 1880. The setting of turquoise gave impetus to the centralized designs with one or more stones as the focus, and later it was also adapted to the overall patterns, such as is found in Zuni "needlepoint" bracelets.

Early Navajo and Zuni work is almost identical and very difficult to tell apart, for the Zunis first learned silversmithing from the Navajos. After the Zunis began to set turquoise in the 1890's their work moved in a different direction towards elaborate use of small stones set in delicate patterns that emulate, in a somewhat heavier style, the Hispanic Mexican filigree work. Of particular note are the earrings with rows of tiny silver and turquoise pendants. The source for these Hispanic style pieces has not been documented, but it is likely a later influence from the New Mexican *plateros* (Hispanic silversmiths) who were making abundant quantities of filigree in the late 1800's and early 1900's

Increased skills and better tools and materials wrought changes in the art among both the Navajos and the Zunis. More highly decorative and perfectly rendered pieces were produced by the Navajos utilizing thinner sheet silver in place of hand-beaten coin and a widely enhanced repertoire of dies for stamping. The Zuni were able to develop their art through the use of the emery wheel for polishing turquoise, the drawplate and small pliers for delicate work, and later, commercially-made silver wire.

The influence of Anglo-American traders was felt not only in technique but also in the rapid commercialization of Indian silverwork which began for the Navajo in the 1890's and for the Zuni considerably later. The large

numbers of commercially-minded Anglo-Americans in the Southwest provided an expanding economy in which better tools and quantities of silver and turquoise were more readily available. Both had previously been in scarce supply, and ultimately, through the medium of the traders, a ready market for Indian jewelry began to develop.

In the beginning this market was small; perhaps the major item of trade was the silver tobacco canteen used by the American soldiers stationed near Navajo territory in the 1870's. The railroad opened the Southwest for tourism and by 1900 a thriving tourist trade was underway. This market made a considerable impact upon Indian, particularly Navajo, jewelry. Traders such as the Fred Harvey Company commissioned lighter pieces, more palatable to Eastern tourists and introduced new design motifs such as arrows and swastikas which were thought to add an "Indian" authenticity to the pieces. After 1900 the making of Indian jewelry was gradually transformed from an indigenous art for the use and pleasure of the makers to an art primarily intended for sale to outsiders. Today it has developed from this relatively simple "tourist" art to an eclectic and wide-ranging art form of remarkable sophistication.

William Wroth
Curator, Taylor Museum
Colorado Springs Fine Arts Center

109 Concha Belt, First Phase, Open Center Type
Navajo, ca. 1880-1900
Conchas are coin silver, buckle is wrought silver with stamped designs.
School of American Research, Santa Fe, Indian Arts Fund Collection

110 *left* **Concha Belt, First Phase, Open Center type**
Navajo, ca. 1880-1890
Conchas are coin silver, buckle is wrought silver with stamped designs.
Private Collection

right **Concha Belt, Second Phase Filed Type**
Navajo, ca. 1890-1900
Conchas are coin silver, buckle is cast.
Private Collection

110

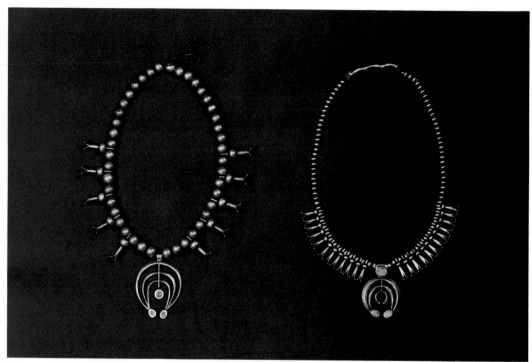

111

111 *left* **Navajo Silver Necklace**
ca. 1890-1910
Cast silver naja with turquoise inlay.
Coin silver beads
Private Collection

right **Navajo Silver Necklace**
ca. 1900-1920
Cast silver naja with turquoise inlay.
Silver beads.
Private Collection

112 *left* **Pueblo Silver Necklace**
ca. 1880-1890
Coin silver crosses and beads
The Taylor Museum at the Colorado
Springs Fine Arts Center

right **Navajo Silver Necklace**
ca. 1870-1890
Cast silver naja; Mexican coin silver beads
The Taylor Museum at the Colorado
Springs Fine Arts Center

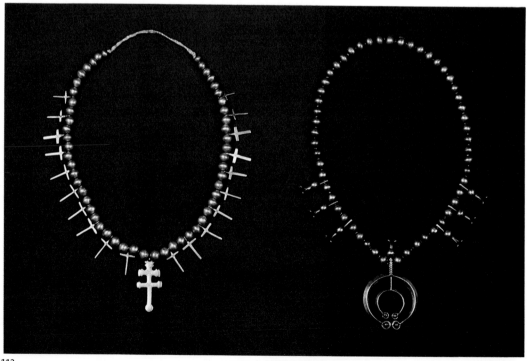

112

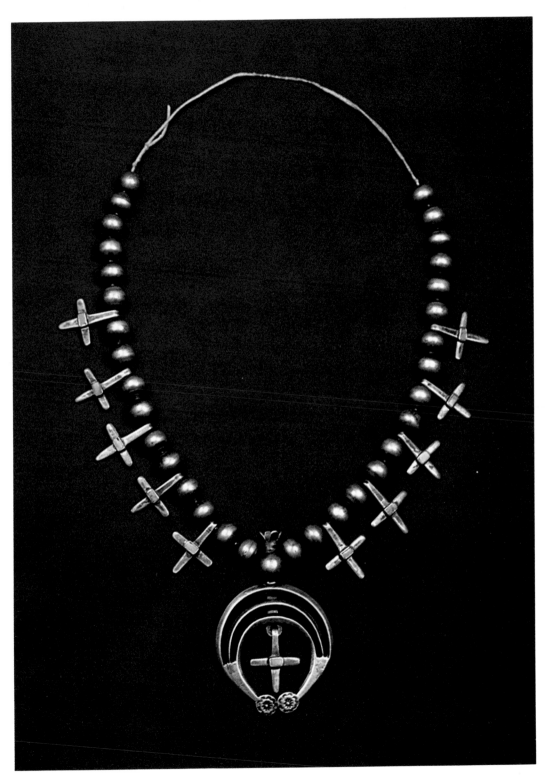

113 Navajo Silver Necklace
ca. 1900-1920
Cast silver naja, coin silver beads and
crosses with turquoise inlay
Private Collection

113

114 *left* **Fetish Necklace**
Zuni, ca. 1880
Turquoise beads with fetishes of shell,
stone, serpentine
Private Collection

right **Shell and Turquoise Necklace**
Navajo or Santo Domingo, ca. 1870
Shell hishi with turquoise nuggets and
shell segments
Private Collection

115 *left* **Shell and Turquoise Necklace**
Pueblo, probably Santo Domingo
ca. 1900
White shell hishi with turquoise nuggets
and shell segments, turquoise inlay shell
suspension
Private Collection

right **Turquoise Necklace**
Navajo (or Pueblo), ca. 1900
Turquoise beads and nuggets; naja is
ironwood with turquoise inlay.
Private Collection

116 *top left* **Navajo Buckle**
ca. 1900-1910
Cast silver and polished turquoise stones
Private Collection

center left **Navajo Dress Ornament**
ca 1900
Polished turquoise stones in silver setting
Private Collection

bottom left **Navajo Buckle**
ca. 1890-1900
Cast silver and polished turquoise stones
Private Collection

top right **Navajo Dress Ornament**
ca. 1900-1910
Polished turquoise in silver setting
Private Collection

bottom right **Navajo Ketoh**
ca. 1890-1900
Cast silver with polished turquoise stones
Private Collection

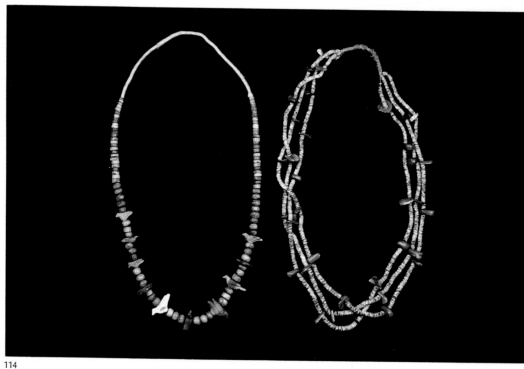

114

115

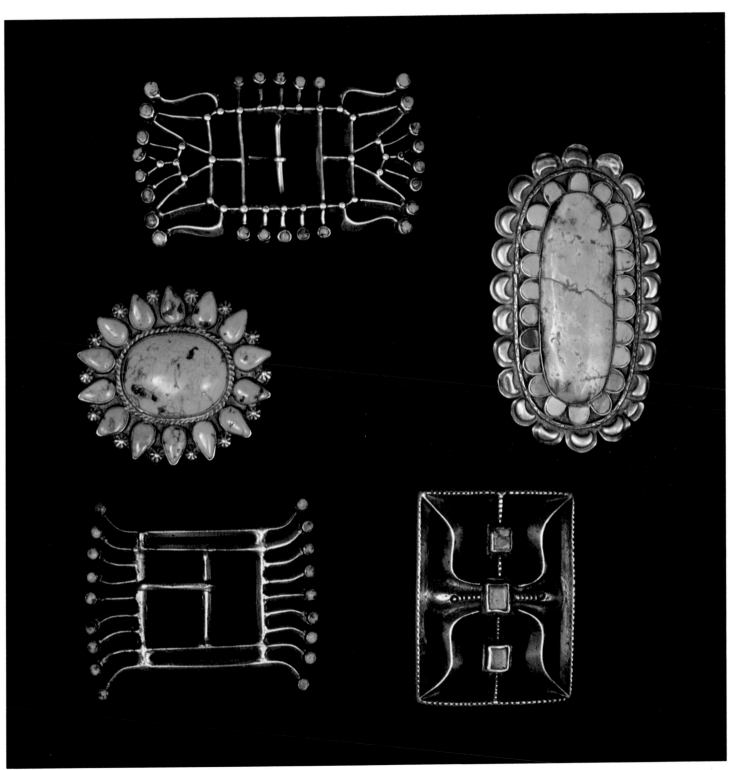

117 *top left* **Zuni "Cluster" Bracelet**
ca. 1900-1920
Polished turquoise stones in silver setting
Private Collection

center left **Navajo Bracelet**
ca. 1890-1910
Cast silver
University of Colorado Museum

bottom left **Navajo Ring**
ca. 1900-1920
Polished turquoise stone in silver setting
Private Collection

top right **Navajo Bracelet**
ca. 1890-1900
Cast silver with polished turquoise stones
University of Colorado Museum

bottom right **Navajo (or Zuni) Bracelet**
ca. 1900-1915
Polished turquoise stones in silver setting
Private Collection

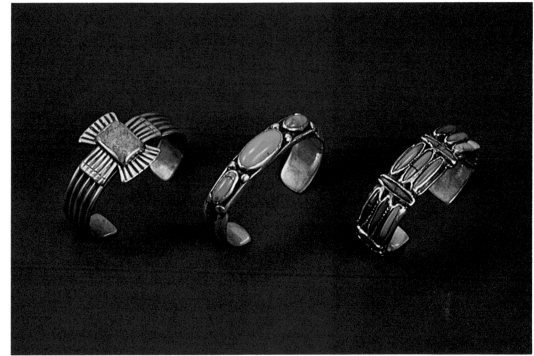

118

118 *left* **Navajo Bracelet**
ca. 1885-1900
Polished turquoise stone in cast silver
setting
Private Collection

center **Navajo Bracelet**
ca. 1900
Polished turquoise stones in silver setting
Private Collection

right **Navajo Bracelet**
ca. 1890-1900
Polished turquoise stones in silver setting
Private Collection

119 *left* **Shell and Turquoise Necklace**
Santa Domingo, ca. 1890-1910
Polished turquoise beads, shell
suspension inlaid with turquoise and jet
Private Collection

right **Shell and Turquoise Necklace**
Pueblo, probably Santo Domingo
ca. 1900-1920
Shell and turquoise beads, suspension is
stamped silver and shell inlaid with
turquoise and jet
University of Colorado Museum

119